STUDY GUIDE

Reformation Truths

Michael Reeves

I0806890

LIGONIER MINISTRIES
Renew your Mind.
LIGONIER.ORG | 800-435-4343

421 Ligonier Court, Sanford, FL 32771
E-mail: info@ligonier.org

Printed in the United States of America.

Contents

Introduction

Many people today dismiss the Reformation as a peculiar chapter of history with little relevance to contemporary life. However, nothing could be further from the truth. In this eight-part teaching series, Dr. Michael Reeves examines the ideas that lay at the heart of the Reformation. Surveying the writings of the brightest Roman Catholic and Protestant scholars of the era, Dr. Reeves reveals the stark contrast between the traditions' very different interpretations of the gospel. By studying the central truths of the Reformation, Christians today can better understand, rejoice in, and proclaim the good news of Jesus Christ.

This study guide is a companion to the video teaching series. Whether you are using the DVDs, streaming the videos on Ligonier.org, or going through the course in Ligonier Connect, this resource is designed to help you make the most of the learning experience. For each message in the series, there is a corresponding lesson in this guide. Here is what you will find in each lesson:

INTRODUCTION	The introduction is a brief paragraph that summarizes the content covered in the lecture and considered in the study guide lesson. **How to use:** Use the introduction to each lesson to get a sense of the big picture before watching the video. Refer to these statements as you work through the study guide to remind you of what you have already covered and where you are headed.
LEARNING GOALS	The learning goals are the knowledge and skills the study guide lesson will endeavor to equip you with as you work through the lecture content. **How to use:** Familiarize yourself with the goals of each lesson before engaging with its contents. Keeping the overall purpose in mind as you watch each video and reflect on or discuss the questions will help you get the most out of each lesson.
KEY IDEAS	The key ideas are the major points or takeaways from the lecture. **How to use:** Use these ideas to prepare yourself for each lesson and to review previous lessons. They describe specifically the knowledge each lecture is communicating.

REFLECTION & DISCUSSION QUESTIONS	The questions are the guided reflection and/or discussion component of the lesson that are intended to help you prepare for, process, and organize what you are learning. **How to use:** Reflect on individually or discuss in a group the questions in the order in which they appear in the lesson. The timestamps in the right margin indicate where the answers to questions during the video can be found.
PRAYER	The prayer section offers suggestions for how to close the lesson in prayer with respect to what was taught in the lecture. **How to use:** Consider using each lesson's prayer section as a guide to personal or group prayer. These sections follow the ACTS prayer model, which you can learn more about in R.C. Sproul's Crucial Questions booklet *Does Prayer Change Things?* This helpful guide is available as a free e-book at Ligonier.org.
REVIEW QUIZ	The review quiz is a set of six multiple-choice questions that appears at the end of each lesson. **How to use:** Use each quiz to check your comprehension and memory of the major points covered in each lecture. It will be most beneficial to your learning if you take a lesson's quiz either sometime between lessons or just before you begin the next lesson in the study guide.
ANSWER KEY	The answer key provides explanations for the reflection and discussion questions and answers to the multiple-choice questions in the review quiz. **How to use:** Use the answer key to check your own answers or when you do not know the answer. Note: Do not give in too quickly; struggling for a few moments to recall an answer reinforces it in your mind.

Study Schedules

The following table suggests four plans for working through the *Reformation Truths* video teaching series and this companion study guide. Whether you are going through this series on your own or with a group, these schedules should help you plan your study path.

	Extended 10-Week Plan	Standard 8-Week Plan	Abbreviated 6-Week Plan	Intensive 4-Week Plan
Week	**Lesson**			
1	*	1	1	1 & 2
2	1	2	2 & 3	3 & 4
3	2	3	4	5 & 6
4	3	4	5	7 & 8
5	4	5	6 & 7	
6	5	6	8	
7	6	7		
8	7	8		
9	8			
10	*			

* For these weeks, rather than completing lessons, spend your time discussing and praying about your learning goals for the study (the first week) and the most valuable takeaways from the study (the last week).

1

Do Words Matter?

INTRODUCTION

Doctrinal clarity and precision are important, but many people today think that the issues of the Reformation were trivial debates over words. In this lecture, Dr. Reeves breaks through common misconceptions about the Reformation to reveal that what was at stake was the gospel itself. By studying the central issues of the Reformation, we will discover that words matter, because theological precision has eternal significance.

LEARNING GOALS

When you have finished this lesson, you should be able to:

- Appreciate the clarity of Reformers' articulation of the gospel
- Explain why doctrinal clarity matters

KEY IDEAS

- The Reformers articulated precise meanings of key doctrines that are central to the Christian gospel.
- A lack of clarity about these essential truths of the faith creates problems in the Christian life.
- Doctrinal clarity can help Christians grow in confidence and Christlikeness.

REFLECTION & DISCUSSION QUESTIONS

Before the Video

What Do You Think?

Take a moment to answer the following questions. They will prepare you for the lecture.

- Why are you undertaking this study?

- What comes to your mind when you think of the Protestant Reformation? In your own words, what was the Reformation mainly about?

Scripture Reading

And the Lord said: "Because this people draw near with their mouth and honor me with their lips, while their hearts are far from me, and their fear of me is a commandment taught by men, therefore, behold, I will again do wonderful things with this people, with wonder upon wonder; and the wisdom of their wise men shall perish, and the discernment of their discerning men shall be hidden."

—Isaiah 29:13–14

- According to this passage, having the right words does not guarantee a right relationship with God. What deeper problems may lurk beneath the veneer of piety?

During the Video

Answer the following questions while you watch the video. They will guide you through the lecture.

Wars over Words? *0:00–9:28*

- What is Dr. Reeves' hope for this teaching series?

- What were the effects of Erasmus' indifference to doctrine?

The Need for Clarity *9:28–20:47*

- How did the answers of evangelical Christians and Roman Catholics compare in the poll taken of believers in the United States and Canada? What problem with the poll does this reveal?

- How did Martin Luther's teaching on assurance of salvation differ from the joint declaration on justification between Roman Catholics and Lutherans in 1999?

After the Video

Answer the following questions after you have finished the lecture. They will help you identify and summarize the major points.

- What is the subtle assumption that may lurk beneath our culture's dismissal of theological issues?

  If you are in a group, have the members identify beliefs for which they would and would not be willing to die.

- In the poll referenced in this lesson, what four statements were used to measure the influence of evangelicalism in Canada and the United States?

  If you are in a group, have the members discuss which of these statements they think most people in our culture would agree with and which they think most people would disagree with. Explain your answers.

- In this lesson, Dr. Reeves said, "As long as doctrine is ignored, we must remain captives of the ruling system or the spirit of the age." Explain this statement.

  If you are in a group, have the members share a specific way that "the spirit of the age" has attempted to hold them captive.

PRAYER

Commit what you have learned from God's Word in this lesson to prayer.

- Praise God for providing a detailed record of His saving work in the Bible.
- Confess areas of carelessness or apathy in your pursuit of biblical truth.
- Thank God for His perfect work as Father, Son, and Holy Spirit in saving you.
- Ask God to give you a greater sense of confidence in and assurance of His saving work in your life.

REVIEW QUIZ

Use these multiple-choice questions to measure what you learned from this lesson.

1. Which of the following scholars said, "The sum of our religion is peace and unanimity"?
   a. Desiderius Erasmus
   b. John Calvin
   c. Mark Noll
   d. Martin Luther

2. Which of the following statements did *not* appear in the poll designed to measure the prominence of evangelicalism in North America?
   a. "I have committed my life to Christ and consider myself to be a converted Christian."
   b. "It is important to encourage non-Christians to become Christians."
   c. "The Bible is the inspired Word of God."
   d. "Through the life, death, and resurrection of Jesus, God provided a way for me to be justified by faith alone."
3. On which date was a joint declaration on justification signed between Lutheran and Catholic leaders?
   a. October 31, 1517
   b. October 31, 1999
   c. October 31, 2000
   d. October 31, 2017
4. The joint declaration of justification upholds the doctrine of assurance as an unassailable article of the Christian faith.
   a. True
   b. False
5. Martin Luther conceded that the issue of ongoing sin calls a believer's assurance of salvation into question.
   a. True
   b. False
6. Which of the following scholars suggested that the Reformation is now over?
   a. Desiderius Erasmus
   b. John Calvin
   c. Mark Noll
   d. Martin Luther

Answer Key—Do Words Matter?

REFLECTION & DISCUSSION QUESTIONS

Before the Video

What Do You Think?

These are personal questions. The answers should be based on your own knowledge and experience.

Scripture Reading

- According to this passage, having the right words does not guarantee a right relationship with God. What deeper problems may lurk beneath the veneer of piety?

  This passage reveals the tragic disconnect that can exist between a person's outward confession and the state of that person's heart. Although an individual may say all the right words about God, that person's heart may be distant from God. Moreover, outward displays of piety may be the result of human rules and traditions rather than a genuine knowledge of and love for God.

During the Video

Wars over Words?

- What is Dr. Reeves' hope for this teaching series?

  The hope is that all who participate in this teaching series will come to appreciate that with the Reformers' clarity on the precise meaning of Reformation truths comes a heightened sense of joy, resolution, and God's power through the gospel.

- What were the effects of Erasmus' indifference to doctrine?

  The kind of doctrinal indifference embodied by the humanist scholar Erasmus exercised an imprisoning, corrosive effect. Erasmus' unwillingness to engage with the deep doctrinal issues of his day meant that he could at best achieve merely cosmetic changes to the medieval Roman Catholic Church. Those who remain indifferent to doctrine have no means of resisting or escaping the prevailing spirit of the age.

The Need for Clarity

- How did the answers of evangelical Christians and Roman Catholics compare in the poll taken of believers in the United States and Canada? What problem with the poll does this reveal?

  In the poll referenced in this lesson, the answers of evangelicals and Roman Catholics were very similar. One-quarter of all respondents who were labeled "evangelical" based on their answers were in fact Roman Catholics. These results indicate that the poll failed to raise any of the issues that were the subject of debate during the Reformation.

- How did Martin Luther's teaching on assurance of salvation differ from the joint declaration on justification between Roman Catholics and Lutherans in 1999?

  This joint declaration takes an ambiguous approach to the topic of assurance. It affirms God's mercy and Christ's merit but also suggests that the assurance of Christians ultimately rests on their own moral discipline. In contrast, Martin Luther insisted that Christians could rest in the unshakable certainty that Christ has taken their sins from them and has imputed His own righteousness to them.

After the Video

- What is the subtle assumption that may lurk beneath our culture's dismissal of theological issues?

  Our culture is quick to dismiss theological issues because of the underlying assumption that the doctrines in question are not actually true. The questions raised in the Reformation concerned significant questions such as, "What will happen to me when I die?" and "How can I know?" An unwillingness to ask important questions like these reveals an underlying attitude of unbelief.

- In the poll referenced in this lesson, what four statements were used to measure the influence of evangelicalism in Canada and the United States?

  The four statements used to determine the presence of evangelical belief in this poll were (1) the Bible is the inspired Word of God; (2) I have committed my life to Christ and consider myself to be a converted Christian; (3) it is important to encourage non-Christians to become Christians; and (4) through the life, death, and resurrection of Jesus, God provided a way for the forgiveness of my sins.

- In this lecture, Dr. Reeves said, "As long as doctrine is ignored, we must remain captives of the ruling system or the spirit of the age." Explain this statement.

  This argument is rooted in the discussion of Erasmus' indifference to deeper doctrinal engagement. Although Erasmus wanted to reform many of the errors and abuses of the medieval Roman Catholic Church, he lacked the theological resources to effect the changes he desired. Problematic religious practice is normally the result of problematic theology. Problematic theology can be dismantled only through a process of rigorous theological reflection and reform. If we are unwilling to engage in this kind of theological enterprise, we will remain trapped in the prevailing errors of our age.

REVIEW QUIZ

Lesson 1

1. **A.**
The sixteenth-century scholar Desiderius Erasmus wrote, "The sum of our religion is peace and unanimity. This can only be when we define as little as possible." In other words, Erasmus considered doctrinal precision an obstacle to peace and unity.

2. **D.**
The four statements used in this poll were (1) the Bible is the inspired Word of God; (2) I have committed my life to Christ and consider myself to be a converted Christian; (3) it is important to encourage non-Christians to become Christians; and (4) through the life, death, and resurrection of Jesus, God provided a way for the forgiveness of my sins. The poll did not bring up the topic of justification or any other contested doctrines of the Reformation.

3. **B.**
Representatives from the Roman Catholic Church and the Lutheran World Federation signed a joint declaration on the doctrine of justification on October 31 (Reformation Day), 1999. This declaration led many observers to conclude that the fundamental theological differences of the Reformation had been resolved.

4. **B.**
The joint declaration on justification takes an ambiguous stance on the doctrine of assurance, ultimately suggesting that the assurance of Christians rests on their own commitment to Jesus Christ.

5. **B.**
Ongoing sin does not call a believer's assurance of salvation into question. Luther wrote that the believer can have full assurance of salvation, noting that "her sins cannot destroy her, since they are laid upon Christ and swallowed up by Him."

6. **C.**
In response to the joint declaration between Lutherans and Roman Catholics on the doctrine of justification, the historian Mark Noll wrote, "If it is true, as once was repeated by Protestants conscious of their anchorage in Martin Luther or John Calvin, that justification is the article on which the church stands or falls, then the Reformation is over." Though premature, this conclusion is easy to reach if one accepts the wording of the joint declaration at face value, without considering the different and incompatible ways that Roman Catholics and Protestants interpret the words of the declaration.

2

The Authority of Scripture

INTRODUCTION

Our view of the Bible can influence every other aspect of our lives. When we view Scripture as irrelevant or as one voice among many, its influence over our lives will be limited. On the other hand, when we recognize God's Word as our final authority, it constantly reforms us. In this lecture, Dr. Reeves will examine the different views of scriptural authority that emerged during the Reformation and will discuss how this issue continues to separate Roman Catholics and Protestants.

LEARNING GOALS

When you have finished this lesson, you should be able to:

- Explain and defend the Reformers' view of biblical authority
- Differentiate between Protestant, Roman Catholic, Mormon, and Muslim views of Scripture

KEY IDEAS

- Scripture alone is the church's ultimate authority for faith and practice.
- The doctrine of *sola Scriptura* places other authorities under the Bible.
- The Bible is trustworthy and proves itself to be what it claims to be: the Word of God.

REFLECTION & DISCUSSION QUESTIONS

Before the Video

What Do You Think?

Take a moment to answer the following questions. They will prepare you for the lecture.

- What are the authorities in your life? How would you rank them in terms of their level of authority over you?

- What specific role does each of these authorities play, and how do they relate to one another?

Scripture Reading

> *And we have the prophetic word more fully confirmed, to which you will do well to pay attention as to a lamp shining in a dark place, until the day dawns and the morning star rises in your hearts, knowing this first of all, that no prophecy of Scripture comes from someone's own interpretation. For no prophecy was ever produced by the will of man, but men spoke from God as they were carried along by the Holy Spirit.*
>
> —2 Peter 1:19–21

- How does Peter articulate the reliability of God's Word in these verses?

During the Video

Answer the following questions while you watch the video. They will guide you through the lecture.

The Issue of Authority *0:00–8:04*

- What is the difference between *sola Scriptura* and *nuda Scriptura*? Why is this difference significant?

- In what way did Erasmus contribute to the Reformation? How did his view of Scripture prevent him from joining the Reformation?

Why Trust the Bible? *8:04–23:48*

- What is the primary reason for us to have confidence in God's Word?

- What does John Calvin mean when he refers to the witness of the Spirit in our recognition of Scripture's authority?

After the Video

Answer the following questions after you have finished the lecture. They will help you identify and summarize the major points.

- Why is it not enough simply to affirm that the Bible is one authoritative voice among many, as opposed to the only final authority in matters of faith and practice? What practical difference does this distinction make in the lives of believers?

  If you are in a group, have the members identify other authorities that tend to compete with Scripture for influence in their lives.

- How did John Owen use the metaphor of light to describe the Bible's authority?

  If you are in a group, have the members share a specific way in which God's Word has provided light and illumination in their lives.

- Do other holy books, such as the Qur'an and the Book of Mormon, authenticate themselves in the same way that the Bible does? Explain your answer.

  If you are in a group, have the members describe ways in which their confidence in the Bible has changed or increased over time.

PRAYER

Commit what you have learned from God's Word in this lesson to prayer.

- Praise God for His sovereign authority over all lesser authorities.
- Confess ways that you resist the authority of God's Word in your life.
- Thank God for giving you His Word as an infallible and trustworthy guide.
- Ask God to help you understand and submit to His Word in a specific area where you are struggling.

REVIEW QUIZ

Use these multiple-choice questions to measure what you learned from this lesson.

1. The medieval Roman Catholic Church affirmed without reservation the authority and inspiration of Scripture.
   a. True
   b. False

2. Which Roman Catholic leader quickly identified final authority as the real issue at stake while debating Martin Luther?
    a. Cardinal Thomas Cajetan
    b. Desiderius Erasmus
    c. Sylvester Prierias
    d. Pope Leo X

3. What did Erasmus publish that helped to fuel the Reformation?
    a. Dutch New Testament
    b. Greek New Testament
    c. Hebrew Old Testament
    d. German New Testament

4. Which of the following best summarizes the principle of *sola Scriptura*?
    a. The Bible is one of many equally valid authorities.
    b. The Bible is inerrant and infallible.
    c. The Bible is the highest authority.
    d. The Bible is the only valid authority.

5. Which of the following best summarizes the principle of Scripture's self-authentication?
    a. Christians come to trust the Bible through a mystical experience.
    b. Scripture can be trusted because it says it can be trusted.
    c. The Bible proves itself to be what it claims to be.
    d. The Bible's superior literary qualities prove that it is true.

6. Who stated, "Scripture seriously affects us only when it is sealed on our hearts through the Spirit"?
    a. Desiderius Erasmus
    b. John Calvin
    c. John Owen
    d. Martin Luther

Answer Key—The Authority of Scripture

REFLECTION & DISCUSSION QUESTIONS

Before the Video

What Do You Think?

These are personal questions. The answers should be based on your own knowledge and experience.

Scripture Reading

- How does Peter articulate the reliability of God's Word in these verses?

  Peter describes the authority of Scripture using the metaphor of a lamp illuminating a dark night, granting visibility until the arrival of the new day. He also affirms that Scripture is of divine origin instead of merely human origin. Due to its inspiration by the Holy Spirit, Scripture speaks with the authority of God Himself.

During the Video

The Issue of Authority

- What is the difference between *sola Scriptura* and *nuda Scriptura*? Why is this difference significant?

  Nuda Scriptura *refers to the idea that Scripture is the only spiritual authority that Christians should recognize. The phrase "no creed but Christ" encapsulates this sentiment. On the other hand, the Reformation principle* sola Scriptura *teaches that other spiritual authorities do exist, but Scripture alone is the Christian's highest authority.* Sola Scriptura *empowers believers to benefit from the guidance of lesser authorities that affirm, clarify, and reinforce the teachings of Scripture.*

- In what way did Erasmus contribute to the Reformation? How did his view of Scripture prevent him from joining the Reformation?

  Erasmus published the first printed edition of the Greek New Testament, effectively giving an entire generation of Bible scholars access to the New Testament in its original language. Although he provided the fuel for the Reformation, he did not participate in it. Believing in the vagueness of Scripture, Erasmus ascribed little practical or governing authority to God's Word. Consequently for Erasmus, the Bible remained one authority among many, which stifled its influence on his thinking and living.

Why Trust the Bible?

- What is the primary reason for us to have confidence in God's Word?

  There are many reasons for confidence in God's Word, but Dr. Reeves points out that the primary reason to trust Scripture is because it is self-authenticating; that is, it proves itself to be what it claims to be.

- What does John Calvin mean when he refers to the witness of the Spirit in our recognition of Scripture's authority?

  In referring to the witness of the Spirit, Calvin is not suggesting that some Christians receive new divine revelation in addition to the Bible. Rather, he is describing the Spirit's process of working in believers to remove their natural spiritual blindness so that they may behold what is already in Scripture.

After the Video

- Why is it not enough simply to affirm that the Bible is one authoritative voice among many, as opposed to the only final authority in matters of faith and practice? What practical difference does this distinction make in the lives of believers?

  If we limit the role of the Bible to that of one voice among many, its power and influence in our lives will be severely limited. Given our nature, these other voices will tend to drown out God's Word and mold its message to fit our own vision of what Christianity should be. On the other hand, when we recognize and submit to the unique authority of God's Word, it begins to mold and shape us according to God's vision of who we should be.

- How did John Owen use the metaphor of light to describe the Bible's authority?

  The great Puritan John Owen observed that Scripture refers to itself as a lamp and a light (Ps. 119:105; 2 Peter 1:19). Owen pointed out that light shines on other things to make them known but does not need anything else to make itself known. Just as light proves itself by what it is, so also God's Word illuminates other things by its truth but does not need any source of illumination other than itself.

- Do other holy books, such as the Qur'an and the Book of Mormon, authenticate themselves in the same way that the Bible does? Explain your answer.

  The Bible is unique in its authentication of itself. When Muslims speak of the Qur'an as self-evidently divine, they are describing the poetic beauty of its literary style. When Mormons describe their trust in the Book of Mormon, they are describing the subjective sense of happiness that they experience when reading it. In contrast, the self-authentication of the Bible is seen not primarily through its literary elegance or through a mystical encounter with God but through its unified, objective, and demonstrable message.

REVIEW QUIZ

Lesson 2

1. **A.**
   In Martin Luther's day, the Roman Catholic Church staunchly affirmed that the Bible is authoritative and inspired by God, as it still teaches today. The Reformers affirmed further that Scripture is the only final *authority for faith and life.*

2. **C.**
   Sylvester Prierias, the first Roman Catholic scholar to respond formally to Martin Luther's ideas, quickly realized that the location of final spiritual authority was the fundamental point of disagreement between Luther and the Roman Catholic Church.

3. **B.**
   In 1516, Erasmus published the first printed edition of the New Testament in Greek, which gave Western Christians widespread access to the New Testament in its original language for the first time in many centuries. It was through Erasmus' Greek New Testament that Martin Luther and other Reformers were able to discover and reclaim crucial biblical truths.

4. **C.**
   In proclaiming the doctrine of sola Scriptura, *the Reformers declared that the Bible alone is the final authority in all matters of faith and practice. Although other secondary authorities, such as creeds, confessions, and tradition, have value, they must be governed by the greater authority of God's Word.*

5. **C.**
   The Reformers argued that Scripture authenticates its own authority. That is, it proves itself to be God's holy Word. We are not to believe it on the basis of its literary qualities or our own subjective experience but because it makes good on its claim to be authoritative and reliable.

6. **B.**
   In his landmark theological work Institutes of the Christian Religion, *John Calvin stated, "Scripture seriously affects us only when it is sealed on our hearts through the Spirit." Calvin's point was that apart from the illuminating work of the Holy Spirit, all people approach God's Word with spiritual blinders on. It is only with the Spirit's help that humanity is enabled to behold and comprehend the riches of God's Word.*

3

The Sinfulness of Man

INTRODUCTION

The biblical view of human sinfulness has never been popular. Both in Martin Luther's day and in our own, the prevailing tendency is to deny the depth and severity of sin in our hearts. While a more optimistic view of human nature may seem to be good news initially, in the long run it leads to greater spiritual enslavement. Only by recovering a biblical understanding of the power of sin in our lives can we begin to find true freedom in Jesus Christ.

LEARNING GOALS

When you have finished this lesson, you should be able to:

- Explain the differences between the Reformation view of sin and other views
- Describe how a radical view of human sin leads to a greater delight in the gospel

KEY IDEAS

- The problem of sin is not merely a behavioral problem; it is a heart problem.
- We don't become righteous by doing righteous deeds; rather, we must be made righteous by God in order to do righteous deeds.
- The radical grace of our Lord Jesus Christ cannot be fully appreciated without a radical understanding of human depravity.

REFLECTION & DISCUSSION QUESTIONS

Before the Video

What Do You Think?

Take a moment to answer the following questions. They will prepare you for the lecture.

- Throughout the course of your life, have you come to see yourself as more sinful or less sinful? Explain your answer.

- How would you describe our culture's view of sin? What aspects of this common perception are accurate, and what aspects of it are inaccurate?

Scripture Reading

The heart is deceitful above all things, and desperately sick; who can understand it? "I the LORD *search the heart and test the mind, to give every man according to his ways, according to the fruit of his deeds."*

—Jeremiah 17:9–10

- According to these verses, what is the natural state of the human heart? How does this passage describe humanity's accountability to God?

During the Video

Answer the following questions while you watch the video. They will guide you through the lecture.

Competing Views of Sin and Righteousness *0:00–11:18*

- According to the Greek philosopher Aristotle, how does a person become righteous?

- How did Martin Luther describe the natural condition of the human will?

The Heart of the Matter *11:18–23:18*

- According to Martin Luther, how can a person cultivate Christ in himself?

- Historically speaking, what has been a consistent mark of times of reformation and revival?

After the Video

Answer the following questions after you have finished the lecture. They will help you identify and summarize the major points.

- In this lesson, Dr. Reeves said, "Sunny stories of how basically good we are, so attractive in their cheeriness, are actually terrible, enslaving lies." Explain this statement. Do you agree or disagree?

  If you are in a group, have the members discuss why they think the narrative that human beings are basically good is so powerful in our culture.

- What metaphors did Erasmus and Luther use to describe the church? What is the fundamental difference between these two approaches to the church?

  If you are in a group, have each member identify which of these two approaches most accurately describes his attitude toward the church in the past. Which approach sounds most liberating?

- Read Genesis 6:5–6. How do these verses describe the problem of human sin? What is God's reaction to sin? Do these verses support Erasmus' view of sin or Luther's?

  If you are in a group, have the members discuss the relationship between sin and grief. What areas of sin and brokenness in the world cause you grief? How do you handle your grief when you sin?

PRAYER

Commit what you have learned from God's Word in this lesson to prayer.

- Praise God for His holy and perfect nature.
- Confess how you fall short of God's holy standards in your thoughts, words, and deeds.
- Thank God for crediting Christ's righteousness to you and giving you a new heart.
- Ask God to help you overcome a specific area of sin in your life.

REVIEW QUIZ

Use these multiple-choice questions to measure what you learned from this lesson.

1. Which of the following best describes Martin Luther's view of sin early in his monastic career?
   a. Luther did not consider sin a serious problem.
   b. Luther identified the regenerating work of the Spirit as the only solution to sin.
   c. Luther regarded sin as a serious problem but not as a deep problem.
   d. Luther staunchly affirmed the doctrine of total depravity.

2. Which of the following documents expressed Martin Luther's challenge to the Aristotelian view of sin and righteousness?
   a. *On the Babylonian Captivity of the Church*
   b. *On the Bondage of the Will*
   c. The Ninety-Five Theses
   d. The Ninety-Seven Theses

3. Which sixteenth-century document argued that sin affects human nature without enslaving it?
   a. *On the Bondage of the Will*
   b. *On the Freedom of the Will*
   c. *The Institutes of the Christian Religion*
   d. *The Manual of the Christian Soldier*

4. According to Erasmus, which of the following best summarizes the problem of sin?
   a. We are dead in our sins.
   b. We are basically good, and sin is merely an illusion.
   c. We are ignorant of the higher truth that brings enlightenment.
   d. We are spiritually sluggish and sleepy.

5. Which of the following metaphors best describes Martin Luther's view of the church?
   a. Army
   b. Body
   c. Family
   d. Vine and branches

6. In the Gospels, which type of person usually shows the greatest love for God?
   a. Gentiles
   b. Pharisees and teachers of the law
   c. Forgiven prostitutes and tax collectors
   d. Pious and respectable middle-class Jews

Answer Key—The Sinfulness of Man

REFLECTION & DISCUSSION QUESTIONS

Before the Video

What Do You Think?

These are personal questions. The answers should be based on your own knowledge and experience.

Scripture Reading

- According to these verses, what is the natural state of the human heart? How does this passage describe humanity's accountability to God?

  Jeremiah 17:9 describes the human heart as deceitful and morally ill. This verse even goes so far as to claim that people do not truly know or understand their own hearts. However, verse 10 confirms that God fully knows the human heart. According to this verse, He searches and tests the desires of every heart and the thoughts of every mind. All people are accountable to Him for their thoughts, desires, and deeds.

During the Video

Competing Views of Sin and Righteousness

- According to the Greek philosopher Aristotle, how does a person become righteous?

  Aristotle taught that a person becomes righteous by doing righteous deeds. According to this view, a persistent commitment to doing righteous acts will eventually produce inward righteousness over time. While incredibly pervasive, Aristotle's message of "self-help" righteousness nevertheless runs against the grain of biblical truth.

- How did Martin Luther describe the natural condition of the human will?

  In his landmark work On the Bondage of the Will, *Luther affirmed that the human will is free to choose in accordance with its desires. However, beneath the surface, the wickedness of the human heart directs and governs what the will desires. Consequently, Luther argued that the will chooses what it wants, but it cannot choose what to want.*

The Heart of the Matter

- According to Martin Luther, how can a person cultivate Christ in himself?

  Martin Luther taught that Christ is cultivated within a person's life through the gospel. According to Luther, faith must spring up and flow from the blood and wounds of Jesus Christ. God's work in the heart through an apprehension of Christ's sacrifice is evidence that He is kindly disposed toward us. As a result of God's work, we grow more and more kindly disposed toward God.

- Historically speaking, what has been a consistent mark of times of reformation and revival?

  Significant periods of reformation and revival in history have been marked by a radical view of human sin. This emphasis features prominently in the ministries of men throughout history such as Martin Luther, John Calvin, George Whitefield, Jonathan Edwards, and the Puritans. We cannot expect a meaningful return to biblical truth in our time unless the need for forgiveness and a new heart is clearly preached.

After the Video

- In this lesson, Dr. Reeves said, "Sunny stories of how basically good we are, so attractive in their cheeriness, are actually terrible, enslaving lies." Explain this statement. Do you agree or disagree?

  The assumption that humanity is basically good implies that a person only needs to try harder and to do more righteous deeds in order to become truly righteous. Sadly, this approach only leads to greater bondage by placing a moral burden on us that we are morally incapable of carrying.

- What metaphors did Erasmus and Luther use to describe the church? What is the fundamental difference between these two approaches to the church?

  Erasmus envisioned the church as an army in which each Christian is expected to obey the rules and do his duty like a good soldier. In contrast, Luther described the church as a family in which Christians are relationally connected to God and to one another. In Erasmus' approach, sin is essentially negligence of duty, and righteousness is a matter of discipline and good works. In Luther's approach, sin is despising and rebelling against the heavenly Father, and righteousness is being reconciled to the Father and receiving adoption into the family of God through the atoning work of Jesus Christ.

- Read Genesis 6:5–6. How do these verses describe the problem of human sin? What is God's reaction to sin? Do these verses support Erasmus' view of sin or Luther's?

  This passage uses the phrase "every intention of the thoughts of his heart" to describe both the comprehensive scope and the inward nature of human sin. These verses show that God was grieved to His heart, not just by the outward manifestations of humanity's sin, but more so on account of the intention of every human heart. Luther's view of sin closely aligns with this passage, while Erasmus' view of sin fails to take the radical fallenness of humanity into account.

REVIEW QUIZ

Lesson 3

1. **C.**
As a young man, Luther's views on sin reflected the medieval church's acceptance of Aristotle's teachings on human nature. As a result, Luther considered sin to be a serious problem that could be addressed by a rigorous commitment to righteous living, but not a deep problem that could only be cured by a sovereign act of God's grace.

2. **D.**
In his Ninety-Seven Theses, released just a few weeks before his more famous Ninety-Five Theses, Luther critiqued the prevailing Aristotelian understanding of human nature. He wrote, "We do not become righteous by doing righteous deeds but, having been made righteous, we do righteous deeds."

3. **B.**
Erasmus articulated his view of human sin in On the Freedom of the Will, *published in 1524. Erasmus acknowledged humanity's problem of sin but denied that the human will is actually enslaved to the power of sin.*

4. **D.**
According to Erasmus' understanding of human sin, our fundamental problem is that we are spiritually sluggish and sleepy. In order to be righteous, sinners simply need to cultivate the inner discipline to achieve the righteousness they are capable of. Sadly, this view grossly underestimates the extent of humanity's radical fallenness.

5. **C.**
For Martin Luther, the church is first and foremost a family. Knowing God as Father is what matters above all. Therefore, sin is not merely a negligence of duty, as Erasmus thought; it is a personal act of relational betrayal against a loving Father.

6. **C.**
The consistent pattern seen in the four Gospels is that those who show the greatest love for God are those who are most aware of the great extent of their own sin and of God's forgiveness. This pattern is demonstrated in Luke 7:36–50.

4

The Grace of God

INTRODUCTION

The depth of God's grace can be difficult to fathom and even harder to believe. Even those who rejoice in the notion of God's grace may at times find themselves living at odds with His grace, subtly drawn more and more to rely on their own good works. In this lecture, Dr. Reeves examines our struggle to come to terms with God's grace and presents a biblical vision of the glorious freedom that God gives to all who come to Him with empty and open hands.

LEARNING GOALS

When you have finished this lesson, you should be able to:

- Explain the difference between salvation by grace and salvation by grace *alone*
- Experience and revel in the freedom and power that God's grace bestows

KEY IDEAS

- The competing doctrines of salvation by grace and salvation by grace *alone* lead to two very different understandings of God's grace.
- The competing doctrines of salvation by grace and salvation by grace *alone* lead to two very different ways of life.
- Experiencing the extravagant grace of God yields true freedom, joy, and spiritual vitality in the life of the Christian.

REFLECTION & DISCUSSION QUESTIONS

Before the Video

What Do You Think?

Take a moment to answer the following questions. They will prepare you for the lecture.

- What gift or act of kindness have you received that has been hardest for you to accept? Why?

- Have you experienced God's grace in a tangible, meaningful way? How did it affect you?

Scripture Reading

For the grace of God has appeared, bringing salvation for all people, training us to renounce ungodliness and worldly passions, and to live self-controlled, upright, and godly lives in the present age, waiting for our blessed hope, the appearing of the glory of our great God and Savior Jesus Christ, who gave himself for us to redeem us from all lawlessness and to purify for himself a people for his own possession who are zealous for good works.

—Titus 2:11–14

- According to this passage, what is the relationship between God's grace and holy living? Whose task is it to purify God's people?

During the Video

Answer the following questions while you watch the video. They will guide you through the lecture.

Saved by Grace or by Grace Alone? *0:00–14:12*

- How did the medieval Roman Catholic Church conceive of salvation by grace?

- How did Luther respond to the common assumption that one will be more loved by God as a result of making oneself more attractive and lovable to God?

Living under Grace Alone *14:12–22:51*

- What concept did Dietrich Bonhoeffer believe was partly to blame for the German church's capitulation to Hitler?

- What realities does God's grace alone enable people to experience when they know themselves to be failures?

After the Video

Answer the following questions after you have finished the lecture. They will help you identify and summarize the major points.

- What is the main difference between the doctrine of salvation by grace as conceived by medieval Roman Catholicism and the doctrine of salvation by grace alone as articulated by the Reformers?

  If you are in a group, have the members describe their first encounter with the grace of God. How would you describe this experience?

- Explain Luther's statement: "The law says, 'Do this,' and it is never done. Grace says, 'Believe in this,' and everything is already done." How does this statement apply to the different views of grace discussed in this lesson?

  If you are in a group, have the members read Romans 5:1–2. What comfort does this passage offer believers who are struggling with doubts about their standing before a holy God?

- How might the doctrine of grace alone be mishandled? How can believers avoid falling into the trap of "cheap grace"?

  If you are in a group, have the members discuss which error poses the greatest risk to them personally: a small view of grace—leading to legalism or works righteousness—or a cheap view of grace—leading to antinomianism or a permissive attitude toward sin.

PRAYER

Commit what you have learned from God's Word in this lesson to prayer.

- Praise God for His grace, which He lavishes on undeserving sinners in Christ.
- Confess your struggles to believe that you are forgiven and to live in the freedom of forgiveness.
- Thank God for uniting you to His Son through the Holy Spirit.
- Ask God to break down barriers in your heart that hinder your acceptance of His grace.

REVIEW QUIZ

Use these multiple-choice questions to measure what you learned from this lesson.

1. When did Martin Luther write "Not because of our merits, salvation is given out of the pure mercy of the promising God"?
   a. As a Roman Catholic monk
   b. As a law student
   c. As a theology student
   d. As a seasoned Reformer

2. Medieval Roman Catholicism believed grace to be a type of force necessary to achieve a righteousness for justification.
   a. True
   b. False

3. What spiritual counsel about grace did Martin Luther give to a friend?
   a. "God helps those who help themselves."
   b. "If you show yourself to be deserving, God will supply what you lack."
   c. "Say, 'You, Lord Jesus, are my righteousness. I am Your sin.'"
   d. "Try harder!"

4. According to Luther's view, grace can be equated with which of the following?
   a. Moral assistance
   b. Antinomianism
   c. Christ Himself
   d. Freedom

5. How did Dietrich Bonhoeffer define the concept of cheap grace?
   a. Grace without boundaries
   b. Grace without Christ
   c. Grace without freedom
   d. Grace without repentance

6. The Reformers believed that one cannot receive the Christ who justifies without receiving the Christ who sanctifies.
   a. True
   b. False

Answer Key—The Grace of God

REFLECTION & DISCUSSION QUESTIONS

Before the Video

What Do You Think?

These are personal questions. The answers should be based on your own knowledge and experience.

Scripture Reading

- According to this passage, what is the relationship between God's grace and holy living? Whose task is it to purify God's people?

  This passage teaches that God's grace precedes a Christian's growth in grace. Rather than qualifying ourselves to receive God's grace through our righteous acts, we receive God's grace and thereby are enabled to turn from our sin, and we begin to grow in holiness. This passage also affirms that Jesus is the One who not only gave Himself for us but who purifies us so that we may become zealous in the pursuit of holiness.

During the Video

Saved by Grace or by Grace Alone?

- How did the medieval Roman Catholic Church conceive of salvation by grace?

  According to medieval Roman Catholicism, God gives grace to those who do what is in their power to be righteous. That is, God saves by grace those who do their best to be worthy of it. In contrast, the Reformers contended that God extends His grace even to the most unworthy.

- How did Luther respond to the common assumption that one will be more loved by God as a result of making oneself more attractive and lovable to God?

  Luther taught that the love of God does not find what is pleasing to Him; it creates it. Instead of seeking out what is already good, God's love bestows good. Therefore, sinners become attractive to God because He loves them. It is not the case that God loves them because they are already attractive to Him.

Living under Grace Alone

- What concept did Dietrich Bonhoeffer believe was partly to blame for the German church's capitulation to Hitler?

  Dietrich Bonhoeffer argued that a mistaken attitude toward grace was partly to blame for the failure of the German church to oppose the Nazi regime. Bonhoeffer wrote a scalding critique of what he called "cheap grace," or "grace without Jesus Christ." Like Bonhoeffer, the Reformers opposed any doctrine of grace that was not rooted in the person and work of Jesus Christ.

- What realities does God's grace alone enable people to experience when they know themselves to be failures?

  All who mourn their own failure and insufficiency can know a new and victorious identity in Christ, assurance of salvation, relief from guilt, and sweet intimacy with an almighty Father who loves them deeply. As a result, they can begin to find in themselves a rising desire to follow the One who is the source of all grace and every good.

After the Video

- What is the main difference between the doctrine of salvation by grace as conceived by medieval Catholicism and the doctrine of salvation by grace alone as articulated by the Reformers?

  According to medieval Roman Catholicism, God's grace provides the extra spiritual boost that Christians need to attain eternal life. However, that grace itself is not a guarantee of eternal life; it merely places salvation within reach for those who will prove themselves worthy. In contrast, the Reformers insisted that salvation depends on grace alone. No combination of grace and works is needed to win God's favor. Instead, the Reformation view of grace recognizes that Christ has already accomplished all that is needed for salvation; sinners need only rely on Him alone to receive the fullness of God's grace and goodness.

- Explain Luther's statement: "The law says, 'Do this,' and it is never done. Grace says, 'Believe in this,' and everything is already done." How does this statement apply to the different views of grace discussed in this lesson?

  The law holds before the sinner an unattainable standard. Any attempt to achieve righteousness under the law heaps an unbearable burden on those who want to be made right with God. The medieval view of grace does little to relieve this burden, as sinners must first demonstrate their worthiness to receive grace and then finish what grace had started. On the other hand, true biblical grace, as understood by the Reformers, removes this burden. The unworthy sinner receives by faith all that he cannot attain on his own. In place of doubt and fear, the redeemed experience joy and freedom.

- How might the doctrine of grace alone be mishandled? How can believers avoid falling into the trap of "cheap grace"?

  The objection to grace that is often raised is this: With the guarantee of God's forgiveness, what is to keep believers from continuing to sin? Paul entertains this objection in Romans 6:1 and responds by turning to the doctrine of union with Christ. Genuine union with Christ brings with it not only release from sin's bondage but also a genuine desire to grow in holiness. To avoid what Bonhoeffer described as "grace without Christ," the Reformers commend Christ Himself; no one receives the Christ who justifies without receiving the Christ who makes us holy.

REVIEW QUIZ

Lesson 4

1. **A.**
While still a devout Roman Catholic monk, Martin Luther affirmed that salvation is given not because of human merit but out of the pure mercy of God. When he wrote these words, Luther remained in complete agreement with the medieval Roman Catholic view of grace.

2. **A.**
Dr. Reeves compared grace in the medieval Roman Catholic view to a force or fuel with which someone can be filled. This is why Roman Catholics can pray, "Hail Mary, full of grace." Grace is the element that enables someone to be justifiable.

3. **C.**
In a letter to a friend, Luther wrote: "My dear brother, learn Christ and Him crucified. Learn to pray to Him and, despairing of yourself, say, 'You, Lord Jesus, are my righteousness. I am Your sin.'"

4. **C.**
According to Luther, grace can be equated with Christ Himself. Luther wrote, "Christ is the divine power, righteousness, blessing, grace, and life." To receive grace alone is to receive Jesus Christ alone.

5. **B.**
Bonhoeffer described "cheap grace" as "grace without Christ." Any experience of grace apart from union with Christ is at best superficial and incomplete, lending itself to moral failure and an ethic characterized by self-interest.

6. **A.**
The Reformers did not regard grace merely as a spiritual commodity, but as the essence of union with Christ. In their understanding, to receive grace is to receive Christ, such that to receive the justifying work of Christ is to receive the sanctifying work of Christ as well.

5

Justified by Faith

INTRODUCTION

Since the Reformation, the doctrine of justification has been famously described as "the article by which the church stands and falls." This doctrine profoundly shapes the way we envision our relationship with God and our approach to the Christian life. In this lesson, Dr. Reeves recounts how Martin Luther's rediscovery of this biblical truth turned his life upside down. By recovering and reclaiming this crucial doctrine today, we too can experience confidence, freedom, and joy.

LEARNING GOALS

When you have finished this lesson, you should be able to:

- Describe how Luther's understanding of and attitude toward God's righteousness changed through his study of God's Word
- Explain the great exchange of the gospel and how it applies to believers
- Experience greater boldness and joy in your relationship with the Lord

KEY IDEAS

- God's righteousness is something that He shares with those who understand their failures, not with those who believe they have sorted themselves out spiritually.
- Righteousness is the result not of moral purification but of God's legal declaration.
- Sin does not undermine the Christian's justification before God.

REFLECTION & DISCUSSION QUESTIONS

Before the Video

What Do You Think?

Take a moment to answer the following questions. They will prepare you for the lecture.

- How would you describe the idea of righteousness to someone who does not know Jesus?

- What thoughts or emotions come to your mind when you think of God as holy, righteous, and just?

Scripture Reading

Blessed is the one whose transgression is forgiven, whose sin is covered. Blessed is the man against whom the Lord *counts no iniquity, and in whose spirit there is no deceit.*

—Psalm 32:1–2

- What distinct phrases does the psalmist use to describe the person who is blessed? What to these phrases reveal about how God deals with sin?

During the Video

Answer the following questions while you watch the video. They will guide you through the lecture.

Luther's Discovery *0:00–13:55*

- Which verse formed the basis for Augustine's understanding of the doctrine of justification? Summarize Augustine's view.

- How did Luther's understanding of the righteousness of God in Romans 1:17 change during his tower experience?

Righteous yet Sinners *13:55–22:11*

- What does the Latin phrase *simul justus et peccator* mean? How is this true of a Christian's life?

- What response did Luther recommend for the devil's accusations against Christians?

After the Video

Answer the following questions after you have finished the lecture. They will help you identify and summarize the major points.

- To whom did Luther cry out when he was caught in a thunderstorm? Why did he address his prayer to that person?

  If you are in a group, have the members identify common obstacles that prevent people from reaching out or drawing near to God. How does the gospel speak to these obstacles?

- How did Luther use the metaphor of a marriage to explain the gospel? In this illustration, what does each spouse share with the other?

  If you are in a group, have the members discuss the spiritual benefits that believers share through our union with Christ. For which of these benefits do you feel most grateful?

- Is it accurate to say that justification gives us a blank slate or makes it as if we have never sinned? Why or why not?

  If you are in a group, have the members respond to the following question: What is the most powerful way that you have experienced freedom in your life as a result of knowing that Jesus has taken away your sin and guilt?

PRAYER

Commit what you have learned from God's Word in this lesson to prayer.

- Praise God for delivering you from your sin and declaring you righteous.
- Confess the areas of sin that remain in your life even after you have been united to Christ.
- Thank God that you may approach Him with honesty and boldness because of your righteous standing before Him.
- Ask God to help you live more consistently with your justification in Christ.

REVIEW QUIZ

Use these multiple-choice questions to measure what you learned from this lesson.

1. Which sixteenth-century scholar described justification as “the first and keenest subject of controversy between us”?
   a. Desiderius Erasmus
   b. John Calvin
   c. Martin Luther
   d. Huldrych Zwingli
2. Which phrase best describes Augustine’s understanding of justification?
   a. The doctrine upon which the church stands or falls
   b. A legal declaration of righteous status
   c. A process of internal transformation
   d. *Simul justus et peccator*
3. Joan of Arc was accused of sinning because she claimed to be which of the following?
   a. Chosen by God
   b. At the same time just and a sinner
   c. Certain of being received into paradise
   d. Justified by faith alone
4. Martin Luther taught that a person could possess a right standing before God and yet sin.
   a. True
   b. False
5. Which of the following best describes the biblical definition of a righteous person?
   a. One who has never sinned
   b. One who had done many good works
   c. One who has experienced moral transformation
   d. One whom God has declared to be righteous
6. According to Dr. Reeves, the doctrine of justification allows sinners to approach a holy God with which of the following?
   a. Awe and wonder
   b. Fear and trembling
   c. Honesty and boldness
   d. Remorse and contrition

Answer Key—Justified by Faith

REFLECTION & DISCUSSION QUESTIONS

Before the Video

What Do You Think?

These are personal questions. The answers should be based on your own knowledge and experience.

Scripture Reading

- What distinct phrases does the psalmist use to describe the person who is blessed? What to these phrases reveal about how God deals with sin?

  This passage describes the blessed person as one "whose transgression is forgiven," "whose sin is covered," "against whom the LORD counts no iniquity," and "in whose spirit there is no deceit." Three of these four phrases describe how God deals with sin. Sin is described as a transgression against God. Yet, this passage affirms that God does forgive transgressions against His law. This forgiveness is possible not because God ignores sin, but because that person's sin has been covered by another. As a result, God no longer counts the iniquity that His people have committed against them.

During the Video

Luther's Discovery

- Which verse formed the basis for Augustine's understanding of the doctrine of justification? Summarize Augustine's view.

  Augustine based his understanding of justification on Romans 5:5, which says, "God's love has been poured into our hearts through the Holy Spirit who has been given to us." Augustine inferred from this passage that justification is the process of God's pouring His love into our hearts, transforming us to be increasingly righteous and therefore increasingly justified. Augustine concluded that justification is a process of internal transformation. The Reformers, on the other hand, understood Romans 5:5 to describe the process of sanctification, which takes place after a person is justified.

- How did Luther's understanding of the righteousness of God in Romans 1:17 change during his tower experience?

  Before his tower experience, Luther hated the phrase "the righteousness of God" in Romans 1:17. For Luther, the concept of God's righteousness was filled with gloom and dread because he knew that God's righteous standard was unattainable for him. Through his tower experience, Luther came to understand that "the righteousness of God" in Romans 1:17 refers to the righteous status that God imputes to sinners as a gift. He came to see God's righteousness as evidence of His love instead of the basis of His judgment.

Righteous yet Sinners

- What does the Latin phrase *simul justus et peccator* mean? How is this true of a Christian's life?

  Luther popularized the phrase simul justus et peccator, *which means "at the same time just and a sinner." This phrase implies that believers remain sinners in themselves while also being righteous in their standing before God. While we continue to experience the effects of our fallenness, we can take heart in the knowledge that God will not count our sins against us (Ps. 32:1–2).*

- What response did Luther recommend for the devil's accusations against Christians?

  Luther urged those who face Satan's accusations to meet these charges head-on with the truth of the gospel. Luther recommended the following response: "I admit I deserve death and hell. What of it? Does this mean I shall be sentenced to eternal damnation? By no means, for I know One who suffered and made satisfaction in my behalf. His name is Jesus Christ, the Son of God. And where He is, there I shall be also."

After the Video

- To whom did Luther cry out when he was caught in a thunderstorm? Why did he address his prayer to that person?

  Luther cried out to Saint Anne for help when he feared that he would be killed in a thunderstorm. Rather than cry out to a holy God who seemed unapproachable to him, Luther chose to direct his prayer to the mother of Mary. He felt that he did not have access to God, but perhaps a request directed through one of the saints would receive a favorable response.

- How did Luther use the metaphor of a marriage to explain the gospel? In this illustration, what does each spouse share with the other?

  Luther explained the gospel through the metaphor of a marriage between a perfect and wealthy king and a destitute prostitute. On their wedding day, each shares with the other all that they have. The king shares his wealth, power, and perfection with his bride. The bride, in turn, shares her debts and shame with her husband, who has more than enough to take on her debts. This illustration represents the great exchange by which Jesus takes on our guilt and shame and imputes to us His perfect righteousness.

- Is it accurate to say that justification gives us a blank slate or makes it as if we have never sinned? Why or why not?

  Christians often think of justification as receiving a spiritual blank slate, of returning to a state of blamelessness as if they had never committed any sin. This understanding is incomplete. Justification not only removes our past and present sins, but also, when God justifies us, He declares us righteous in Christ. We are in full possession of Christ's righteousness and have no need of being "re-justified" for any future mistakes we will make or any future sins we will commit. Our future sins are covered by Christ's righteousness as much as our past and present sins. If we are in Christ, there is no longer any condemnation for us now, nor will there ever be (Rom. 8:1).

REVIEW QUIZ

Lesson 5

1. **B.**
   Calvin described the doctrine of justification as "the first and keenest subject of controversy between us." This statement highlights the fact that different views of the doctrine of justification lead to very different views of the gospel and the Christian life.

2. **C.**
   For Augustine, justification was a process of internal transformation. He interpreted Romans 5:5 as a summary statement of salvation, in which God gradually pours His love into human hearts.

3. **C.**
   One of the charges brought against Joan of Arc at her trial in 1531 was, "This woman sins when she says she is certain of being received into paradise." The rationale behind this charge was the belief that no one can know whether he is worthy of glory or punishment. In medieval Roman Catholicism, the notion of assurance of salvation was considered prideful, misguided, or even blasphemous.

4. **A.**
   In his famous statement simul justus et peccator, *Martin Luther affirmed two biblical truths: (1) Christians hold a blameless moral standing in God's eyes; and (2) Christians continue to sin even after being declared righteous by God.*

5. **D.**
   The Bible teaches that a righteous person is not one who has never sinned or who has done a multitude of good works; the righteous person is the sinner on whom God has pronounced the verdict "righteous."

6. **C.**

In his conclusion to this lesson, Dr. Reeves celebrates the fact that the reality of justification permits us to approach a holy God with absolute honesty about our failure and absolute boldness because we share Christ's righteousness before the Father. Although the other attributes listed are appropriate responses to God, they are less grounded in the doctrine of justification.

6

Union with Christ

INTRODUCTION

In this lesson, Dr. Reeves will examine a doctrine that is sometimes neglected in discussions about Reformation theology: union with Christ. This doctrine is at the very heart of the gospel. When sinners are joined to Jesus Christ, sharing in His death and resurrection, the vast riches of the gospel become theirs. Examining this crucial article of faith is an invitation to rejoice in a glorious Reformation truth.

LEARNING GOALS

When you have finished this lesson, you should be able to:

- Identify several Scripture passages that describe the Christian's union with Christ
- Describe the role of each person of the Trinity in uniting sinners to Jesus Christ
- Explain the practical significance of the doctrine of union with Christ to the life of the believer

KEY IDEAS

- Union with Christ marks the starting point, not the endpoint, of the Christian life.
- Union with Christ is the means by which Christ's benefits are shared with believers.
- Union with Christ gives the guilty sinner a glorious and unshakable new identity.

REFLECTION & DISCUSSION QUESTIONS

Before the Video

What Do You Think?

Take a moment to answer the following questions. They will prepare you for the lecture.

- What comes to mind when you think of the words *unity*, *union*, or *united*?

- Why is it important to have union with Christ?

Scripture Reading

> *For if we have been united with him in a death like his, we shall certainly be united with him in a resurrection like his. We know that our old self was crucified with him in order that the body of sin might be brought to nothing, so that we would no longer be enslaved to sin. For one who has died has been set free from sin. Now if we have died with Christ, we believe that we will also live with him. We know that Christ, being raised from the dead, will never die again; death no longer has dominion over him. For the death he died he died to sin, once for all, but the life he lives he lives to God. So you also must consider yourselves dead to sin and alive to God in Christ Jesus.*
>
> —Romans 6:5–11

- According to Romans 6:5–11, what are the results of being united with Jesus Christ?

During the Video

Answer the following questions while you watch the video. They will guide you through the lecture.

Catalyst or Goal? *0:00–7:42*

- How did the medieval theologian Bernard of Clairvaux envision union with Christ taking place?

- According to John Calvin, how does union with Christ relate to the larger picture of the Christian life?

A Shared Status *7:42–20:33*

- In what sense did the Reformation represent a Copernican revolution in theology?

- How did Calvin respond to the concern that the doctrine of assurance would remove motivation to live a holy life?

After the Video

Answer the following questions after you have finished the lecture. They will help you identify and summarize the major points.

- According to the Reformers, how is union with Christ different from communion with Christ?

  If you are in a group, have the members discuss how their enjoyment of Christ fluctuates over time. When have you felt particularly close to Jesus? When have you felt unusually distant from Him?

- What does the metaphor of the vine and the branches in John 15:1–11 teach about the importance of union with Christ?

  If you are in a group, have the members discuss their experiences of being grafted into Jesus Christ. How does your union with Christ make a difference in daily living?

- How can the doctrine of union with Christ operate as a safeguard against both pride and despair?

  If you are in a group, have the members discuss the following questions: In which areas of your life are you most vulnerable to the temptation of pride? In which areas do you grow most easily discouraged? How does your identity in Christ change the way you see yourself in these areas?

PRAYER

Commit what you have learned from God's Word in this lesson to prayer.

- Praise the Father for sending the Spirit to unite you to the risen and glorious Son.
- Confess times when you have neglected your communion with Jesus Christ.
- Thank God for the life of Christ that is at work in you to make you a new creation.
- Ask God to work in the hearts of the lost so that they, too, may experience union with Christ.

REVIEW QUIZ

Use these multiple-choice questions to measure what you learned from this lesson.

1. One of the major doctrinal discoveries of the Reformation was the concept of the church as the bride of Christ in union with Him.
   a. True
   b. False

2. Which of the following theologians stated that "union [with Christ] is the foundation of communion [with Christ]"?
   a. Bernard of Clairvaux
   b. John Calvin
   c. Richard Sibbes
   d. John Owen

3. According to Romans 5:12, an individual's problem with sin began with which of the following?
   a. Birth
   b. Adam
   c. His first sin against God
   d. The temptation of Eve

4. Which of the following constitutes the center of Reformation theology?
   a. Authority of Scripture
   b. Justification by faith alone
   c. Salvation by grace alone
   d. Jesus Christ

5. Which theologian was fond of identifying himself as a lover of Jesus Christ?
   a. Bernard of Clairvaux
   b. John Calvin
   c. Richard Sibbes
   d. John Owen

6. In the analogy of the vine and the branches, which of the following did Dr. Reeves say would be representative of the Holy Spirit?
   a. A branch
   b. A leaf
   c. The sap
   d. The vine

Answer Key—Union with Christ

REFLECTION & DISCUSSION QUESTIONS

Before the Video

What Do You Think?

These are personal questions. The answers should be based on your own knowledge and experience.

Scripture Reading

- According to Romans 6:5–11, what are the results of being united with Jesus Christ?

  In this passage, Paul declares that believers are united to Jesus in both His death and His resurrection. Our old selves have been crucified with Christ and buried with Him so that our old desires, sins, and failures might be put to death. Because we have also been raised with Jesus, we now experience a new life in which sin and death no longer exercise dominion over us. His victory is our victory.

During the Video

Catalyst or Goal?

- How did the medieval theologian Bernard of Clairvaux envision union with Christ taking place?

  Bernard of Clairvaux envisioned union with Christ as a fluid state that Christians could experience to varying degrees. Bernard longed to experience a deeper state of union with Christ and believed that through many tears, prayers, and sacraments, the Christian could draw ever closer to Christ until attaining perfect union with Him.

- According to John Calvin, how does union with Christ relate to the larger picture of the Christian life?

  While Bernard of Clairvaux imagined the Christian life as a process of striving toward union with Christ, Calvin understood union with Christ to be the starting point of the Christian life. In Calvin's view, the Christian life is a process of living out this union with Christ, not of striving to attain it.

A Shared Status

- In what sense did the Reformation represent a Copernican revolution in theology?

  Just as the Copernican revolution in astronomy identified the true center of the solar system, so the Protestant Reformation identified the true center point of theological truth. The fallen human tendency is to place oneself at the center of one's life, resulting in a distorted, man-centered approach to the Christian life. Instead, the Reformation placed Christ back at the center of theology and the Christian life.

- How did Calvin respond to the concern that the doctrine of assurance would remove motivation to live a holy life?

  In spite of concerns that the doctrine of assurance was too comforting and would give people license to go on sinning, Calvin understood the theological reality of union with Christ to be a natural safeguard against this tendency. Since believers enter a spiritual union with Christ, who is holy, the Spirit of holiness lays hold of and transforms believers, moving them to love and desire what Christ desires.

After the Video

- According to the Reformers, how is union with Christ different from communion with Christ?

  The Reformers understood union with Christ to be a fixed, stable reality that believers experience when they are born again. This union is permanent and unshakable. However, a believer's communion with Christ, otherwise described as the enjoyment of the relationship with Him, can be fluid and wavering. Because of this distinction, Christians can take heart that even when they feel distant from Jesus, nothing can jeopardize their status as children of God and co-heirs with Christ.

- What does the metaphor of the vine and the branches in John 15:1–11 teach about the importance of union with Christ?

  Calvin understood Jesus' teaching on the vine and the branches to be a helpful image of the believer's union with Christ. Jesus is the vine filled with the love and life of God. Unattached to Jesus, we are devoid of spiritual life. Once the Holy Spirit grafts us into the vine, we begin to experience the very life of Christ within us. As Calvin concluded, there is no gospel apart from union with Christ.

- How can the doctrine of union with Christ operate as a safeguard against both pride and despair?

  Our natural tendency is to base our identity on our own performance. When we seem to be doing well on our own strength, we can easily fall into the trap of pride. When our identity rests in ourselves and we are doing poorly, we can easily succumb to a feeling of despair. However, when we place our identity in the union that we share with Jesus Christ, our response becomes one of confidence in the unshakable status of Jesus that has been imputed to us and one of humility grounded in the fact that all that we have is because of Jesus' works and not our own.

REVIEW QUIZ

Lesson 6

1. **B.**
Christians of every generation and theological stripe have embraced the concept of union with Christ as part of the gospel. Views on what exactly this union means and how it is experienced have varied significantly over the centuries.

2. **C.**
Speaking of the believer's relationship with Jesus Christ, the Puritan theologian Richard Sibbes wrote, "Union is the foundation of communion." In other words, the Christian's union with Jesus Christ is the fixed reality that enables us to experience lasting joy in Him.

3. **B.**
In Romans 5:12, Paul explains that sin entered the world through one man, Adam. In Adam, all people sinned, and through Adam, death spread to all of humanity. In the verses that follow, Paul goes on to explain that grace came through Jesus Christ, the second Adam.

4. **D.**
The Reformation placed Jesus Christ at the center of theology. For this reason, Dr. Reeves describes the Reformation as a true Copernican revolution in theology.

5. **B.**
As a young believer, Calvin began to identify himself as "a lover of Jesus Christ." Calvin understood and affirmed that the greatest reward of union with Christ is Christ Himself.

6. **C.**
In the analogy of the vine and branches (John 15:1–11), Jesus declared that He is the vine and His followers are the branches. Implicit in this analogy is the reality that the Holy Spirit functions as the sap, which Christ pours into us to give us life and make us fruitful.

7

Experiencing the New Birth

INTRODUCTION

Many Christians experience uncertainty when it comes to understanding and relating to the Holy Spirit. Although our theology tells us that the Holy Spirit is the third person of the Trinity, we may not always know how to connect this truth to the reality of our day-to-day lives. In this lecture, Dr. Reeves presents a helpful overview of the person and work of the Holy Spirit and the Reformers' understanding that the Spirit is at the very heart of the gospel.

LEARNING GOALS

When you have finished this lesson, you should be able to:

- Describe how and why the Spirit is essential to the Christian life
- Articulate a multifaceted theology of the Holy Spirit

KEY IDEAS

- The Spirit is at the very heart of Reformed theology.
- The Spirit brings about the heart change that is necessary for faith in Christ.
- The Spirit enables Christ-centered holiness instead of lifeless and superficial good works.

REFLECTION & DISCUSSION QUESTIONS

Before the Video

What Do You Think?

Take a moment to answer the following questions. They will prepare you for the lecture.

- When you think of the Holy Spirit, what ideas come to mind?

- How have you experienced the work of the Holy Spirit in your own life? How have you seen the Spirit work in the lives of others?

Scripture Reading

> *Jesus answered, "Truly, truly, I say to you, unless one is born of water and the Spirit, he cannot enter the kingdom of God. That which is born of the flesh is flesh, and that which is born of the Spirit is spirit. Do not marvel that I said to you, 'You must be born again.' The wind blows where it wishes, and you hear its sound, but you do not know where it comes from or where it goes. So it is with everyone who is born of the Spirit."*
>
> —John 3:5–8

- What do these words of Jesus tell us about the work of the Holy Spirit?

During the Video

Answer the following questions while you watch the video. They will guide you through the lecture.

The Reformation Battle for the Doctrine of the Spirit *0:00–14:08*

- According to Dr. Reeves, the Reformation could be described as a fight for which line from the Nicene Creed? What does this particular line from the creed imply?

- What role in salvation did William Tyndale ascribe to the Holy Spirit?

Reclaiming the Reformation Doctrine of the Spirit Today *14:08–22:08*

- Why is the Reformers' theology of the Spirit important today?

- How does the Holy Spirit connect to the five *solas* of the Reformation?

After the Video

Answer the following questions after you have finished the lecture. They will help you identify and summarize the major points.

- How did the work of the Holy Spirit end up being overshadowed in medieval Roman Catholicism?

  If you are in a group, have the members discuss how the person and work of the Holy Spirit are spoken of in Christianity today. In what ways is the Spirit still overshadowed? In what ways is He recognized and celebrated?

- What is the difference between "explicit faith" and "implicit faith" as expressed in medieval Roman Catholicism?

  If you are in a group, have the members discuss the prevalence of "implicit" and "explicit" faith today. Which one of these approaches to salvation is most common in today's culture? How would most people you know define the concept of faith?

- What is ritualism? How is it still pervasive in the church today?

  If you are in a group, have the members identify and share examples of how this tendency toward ritualism creeps into their own spiritual lives.

PRAYER

Commit what you have learned from God's Word in this lesson to prayer.

- Praise God for His sovereign and beautiful work through the Holy Spirit in carrying out His redemptive purposes.
- Confess ways that you have neglected the Spirit's work in your life.
- Thank God for breathing His life into you by the power of the Holy Spirit.
- Ask God to purify your heart through the Spirit so that you might bear righteous fruit for God's glory.

REVIEW QUIZ

Use these multiple-choice questions to measure what you learned from this lesson.

1. The statement "We believe in the Holy Spirit, the Lord, the giver of life" appears in which of the following doctrinal documents?
   a. Apostles' Creed
   b. Heidelberg Catechism
   c. Nicene Creed
   d. Westminster Confession of Faith

2. Which of the following best summarizes Luther's view of the Spirit's role in salvation?
   a. The Spirit cooperates with human effort.
   b. The Spirit inspires sinners to take the initiative in spiritual matters.
   c. The Spirit provides spiritual assistance to weak sinners.
   d. The Spirit raises the dead to spiritual life.

3. Which theologian said, "Our problem is the heart with all the powers, affections, and appetites wherewith we can only sin"?
   a. John Calvin
   b. Martin Luther
   c. Richard Sibbes
   d. William Tyndale
4. The Reformers taught that outward acts of sin are manifestations of the inner desires of the heart.
   a. True
   b. False
5. Which of the following was Luther's preferred title for the Holy Spirit in his hymns?
   a. Breath of God
   b. Comforter
   c. Giver of Life
   d. Paraclete
6. The Reformers' theology of the Holy Spirit encompassed all except for which of the following spiritual benefits?
   a. Assurance of salvation
   b. Deep heart metamorphosis
   c. Personal communion with God
   d. Superficial behavior modification

Answer Key—Experiencing the New Birth

REFLECTION & DISCUSSION QUESTIONS

Before the Video

What Do You Think?

These are personal questions. The answers should be based on your own knowledge and experience.

Scripture Reading

- What do these words of Jesus tell us about the work of the Holy Spirit?

  In this passage, Jesus underscores the importance of the Holy Spirit's work in the salvation of fallen sinners. Entrance into God's kingdom is impossible apart from the Spirit's work in bringing about a second birth. Just as the movement of the wind is mysterious and independent of all human control, so also the life-giving work of the Holy Spirit is imperceptible to human eyes and independent of human effort or control. God's Spirit acts sovereignly and mysteriously to bring about the conversion of God's people.

During the Video

The Reformation Battle for the Doctrine of the Spirit

- According to Dr. Reeves, the Reformation could be described as a fight for which line from the Nicene Creed? What does this particular line from the creed imply?

  Dr. Reeves notes that in many ways the Reformation was a fight for the creedal statement, "We believe in the Spirit, the Lord, the giver of life." That line from the creed assumes that we do not have life in ourselves. Rather, we are utterly dependent on the Spirit to breathe new spiritual life into us.

- What role in salvation did William Tyndale ascribe to the Holy Spirit?

  William Tyndale, the Reformer known for translating the Bible into English, recognized that all sinners have a fundamental heart problem and are therefore trapped in sin. According to Tyndale, "The only solution is the Spirit which looseth the heart." Tyndale understood that no one can be saved apart from the regenerating work of the Holy Spirit.

Reclaiming the Reformation Doctrine of the Spirit Today

- Why is the Reformers' theology of the Spirit important today?

  Dr. Reeves points out that Christians today continue to experience a strong gravitational pull away from knowing God. Many tend to approach Christianity as a matter of going to church, living a moral life, and obtaining a "get out of hell free" card, without actually knowing and communing with Jesus Christ. For this reason, a robust theology of the Holy Spirit is just as desperately needed today as it was five centuries ago.

- How does the Holy Spirit connect to the five *solas* of the Reformation?

  The Reformers' theology of the Holy Spirit permeated all other areas of Reformation theology: (1) since the Spirit is the giver of live, salvation must be by grace alone; (2) since the Spirit of adoption freely unites us to Christ, salvation is by faith alone in Christ alone; (3) since the Spirit enables us to know God the Father with the security of the Son, salvation is through Christ alone by faith alone through grace alone; (4) since the Spirit prevents us from placing any other authority over the Bible, Scripture alone must be our highest authority; (5) since the Spirit applies to sinners the redemptive work decreed by the Father and accomplished by the Son, and since the Spirit moves our hearts to exalt Christ as Lord, then salvation is for the glory of God alone.

After the Video

- How did the work of the Holy Spirit end up being overshadowed in medieval Roman Catholicism?

  In medieval Roman Catholicism, a sophisticated sacramental system emerged in which the clergy were understood as regulating God's grace and administering it to the common people. In effect, there was nothing left for the Spirit to do.

- What is the difference between "explicit faith" and "implicit faith" as expressed in medieval Roman Catholicism?

  According to the medieval Roman Catholic Church, a clear statement of personal trust in Jesus Christ as Savior and Lord is "explicit faith," a commendable but unnecessary verbal confession of belief. The church believed that all that is needed for salvation is merely a demonstration of "implicit faith," faith demonstrated by outward actions but not explicitly defined. As a result, the church considered it unnecessary to verbally confess Jesus as Lord because participation in the sacraments was considered sufficient evidence of faith for the uneducated and illiterate.

- What is ritualism? How is it still pervasive in the church today?

  Dr. Reeves describes ritualism as the notion that religious practices and rituals bring grace simply through the performance of them. This tendency is no less pervasive in the church today than it was five hundred years ago. Examples of ritualism include the contemporary self-help trend and the impulse to busy oneself with a flurry of spiritual activities.

REVIEW QUIZ

Lesson 7

1. **C.**
   After describing the person and work of Jesus Christ with great care and precision, the Nicene Creed begins its summary of the person and work of the Holy Spirit with this affirmation: "We believe in the Holy Spirit, the Lord, the giver of life." Implicit in this statement is the assumption that believers are spiritually dead apart from the Spirit's life-giving work.

2. **D.**
   Luther acknowledged that sinners cannot believe in Jesus Christ through their own strength or reason. He affirmed that the Holy Spirit is the One who calls believers to faith in Christ. The Holy Spirit's work is therefore best understood as God's divine act of raising the dead to spiritual life.

3. **D.**
   The Reformer and English Bible translator William Tyndale understood that humanity's sin problem is not merely superficial but is a problem of the heart. In this statement, Tyndale affirms that lost sinners have no recourse except for "the Spirit which looseth the heart."

4. **A.**
   The Reformers believed that the root of humanity's problem is not sinful behavior. Rather, sinful behavior is a symptom of the underlying problem of sinful desires. Any meaningful change in outward behavior must originate in a changed heart.

5. **B.**
   Martin Luther wrote hymns prolifically as a means of teaching his congregation to worship the Lord through song. The title that Luther used most often to describe the Holy Spirit in his hymnody was "Comforter."

6. **D.**
   The Reformers presented a robust theology of the Holy Spirit, which emphasized numerous aspects of the Spirit's work: deep heart metamorphosis instead of superficial behavior change; personal communion with God instead of abstract blessing; joy in the Lord instead of lifeless ritualism; and assurance of salvation instead of fearful works righteousness.

8

Seeking God's Glory

INTRODUCTION

Reformation theology is more than an abstract set of Scriptural tenets. Rather, it is a coherent and comprehensive framework for thinking, living, and worship that is united around a central theme. Without the beautiful and compelling nucleus of the sovereign goodness and majesty of God, Reformed theology would lose its heart and soul. In this lesson, Dr. Reeves turns our attention to this magnificent core of Christianity: the joy-laden pursuit of the glory of God.

LEARNING GOALS

When you have finished this lesson, you should be able to:

- Summarize the Reformers' view on the source of meaning and purpose in life
- Explain how the topics of comfort, joy, and eternal life helped start the Reformation
- Describe what makes the Reformed faith different from all other approaches to God

KEY IDEAS

- The glory of God is the central focus of Reformed theology and faithful Christian living.
- Beholding and worshiping God for who He is makes human life rich, full, and happy.

REFLECTION & DISCUSSION QUESTIONS

Before the Video

What Do You Think?

Take a moment to answer the following questions. They will prepare you for the lecture.

- What experiences in life have brought you the most joy? What role did God play in these experiences?

- How do you think most people would respond to the question, What is the meaning of life? How do these common answers compare with what you have learned about Reformation theology?

Scripture Reading

Now to him who is able to do far more abundantly than all that we ask or think, according to the power at work within us, to him be glory in the church and in Christ Jesus throughout all generations, forever and ever. Amen.

—Ephesians 3:20–21

- How is the power and majesty of God displayed in these verses?

During the Video

Answer the following questions while you watch the video. They will guide you through the lecture.

Confident of Our Salvation *0:00–7:00*

- What two truths functioned as the guiding lights of the Reformation?

- What did medieval Roman Catholicism believe about the idea that Christians can have assurance of salvation?

Reclaiming Joy and God's Glory *7:00–22:21*

- How did the question of what happens after death play a significant role in the Reformation?

- According to John Calvin, how does the doctrine of purgatory undermine God's glory?

After the Video

Answer the following questions after you have finished the lecture. They will help you identify and summarize the major points.

- How did C.S. Lewis modify the notion of purgatory to make it more consistent with Reformation beliefs? What difficulty remains with this version of purgatory?

  If you are in a group, have the members discuss the idea of trying to grow in spiritual maturity outside of fellowship with God and His people. How successful would this kind of attempt be? Why?

- According to Dr. Reeves, what is the litmus test of truly Reformed thought?

  If you are in a group, have the members discuss how this litmus test can be applied to other aspects of your life. Based on this test, what is an area of your life that is in need of reformation?

- According to Reformation theology, what is the chief end, or defining purpose, of human existence? How can the study of key Reformation truths equip Christians to pursue this purpose?

  If you are in a group, have the members reflect on this teaching series. How has God challenged your thinking during this study? Which of these Reformation truths has had the most significant impact on you?

PRAYER

Commit what you have learned from God's Word in this lesson to prayer.

- Praise God that He is the sovereign ruler of all things and that He alone is worthy of your awe and adoration.
- Confess your tendency to stray from a God-centered focus to a self-centered focus.
- Thank God for His loving desire to bring you joy through intimate union with Him.
- Ask God to help you and others glorify Him and enjoy Him forever.

REVIEW QUIZ

Use these multiple-choice questions to measure what you learned from this lesson.

1. According to Richard Sibbes, which doctrine is prerequisite to many of the duties that God requires?
   a. Assurance of salvation
   b. Inerrancy of Scripture
   c. Total depravity
   d. Sanctification
2. Which of the following emotions does the Heidelberg Catechism associate with the expectation of Christ's return to judge the living and the dead?
   a. Fear
   b. Apathy
   c. Comfort
   d. Longing
3. All except for which of the following were examples of the medieval purgatory industry?
   a. Chantries
   b. Indulgences
   c. Inquisitions
   d. Prayers and Masses for the dead
4. Which of the following men was heavily involved in the sale of indulgences?
   a. Desiderius Erasmus
   b. Johann Tetzel
   c. Martin Luther
   d. Richard Sibbes
5. According to "The Dream of Gerontius," in what context does the soul experience the spiritual transformation necessary for heaven?
   a. At the foot of the cross
   b. In a state of seclusion and absence from God
   c. In the awe-inspiring presence of God's holiness
   d. While fully engaged in God's mission in the world
6. Which of the following best describes John Calvin's view of man's "chief good"?
   a. Glorifying God and enjoying Him forever
   b. The true happiness found within us
   c. Knowledge of learned philosophers
   d. Union with God

Answer Key—Seeking God's Glory

REFLECTION & DISCUSSION QUESTIONS

Before the Video

What Do You Think?

These are personal questions. The answers should be based on your own knowledge and experience.

Scripture Reading

- How is the power and majesty of God displayed in these verses?

  In these verses, Paul articulates God's omnipotence in terms of His capacity "to do far more abundantly than all that we ask or think." Additionally, God's sovereign work is carried out "according to the power at work within us," describing the activity of the Holy Spirit in conforming believers to the image of Jesus Christ. Moreover, the central thrust of this passage is the glory that rightfully belongs to God for his work "in the church and in Christ Jesus," "throughout all generations," and "forever and ever."

During the Video

Confident of Our Salvation

- What two truths functioned as the guiding lights of the Reformation?

  The twin truths that were the guiding lights of the Reformation were the glory of God and His people's enjoyment of Him. The Reformers believed that in all the doctrines they upheld and fought for that God would be more glorified and His people would be given greater comfort and joy. The doctrine of justification by grace alone through faith alone in Christ alone exalts God as utterly merciful and good, and through this doctrine, His people can experience the delight of a firm standing and intimate relationship with Him.

- What did medieval Roman Catholicism believe about the idea that Christians can have assurance of salvation?

  Assurance of salvation was condemned as a sin of presumption by Roman Catholic theology. According to medieval Roman Catholicism, one could only have as much confidence in heaven as one could have in his own ability and performance. This attitude toward salvation left people in the church terrified by the thought of God's judgment.

Reclaiming Joy and God's Glory

- How did the question of what happens after death play a significant role in the Reformation?

  The issue that prompted Martin Luther to write the Ninety-Five Theses in October 1517 was the doctrine of purgatory, which directly deals with of what happens to the believer after death. Luther's passion to help Christians experience comfort and confidence in the face of death sparked the initial event that set the Reformation in motion.

- According to John Calvin, how does the doctrine of purgatory undermine God's glory?

  In the eyes of the Reformers, the doctrine of purgatory symbolized all that was wrong with the medieval Roman Catholic view of salvation. Calvin said, "What remains but to say that purgatory is simply a dreadful blasphemy against Christ!" Calvin contended that purgatory, with its emphasis on the saving power of human action, stripped Christ of His glory as a merciful and fully sufficient savior.

After the Video

- How did C.S. Lewis modify the notion of purgatory to make it more consistent with Reformation beliefs? What difficulty remains with this version of purgatory?

  C.S. Lewis envisioned the possibility of a form of purgatory that was not a place of punishment for remaining spiritual debt but rather a sort of spiritual school where those who are already forgiven can go "to be fully holy and fit for heaven." While this form of purgatory avoids the problem of presenting Christ's atonement as insufficient, it creates another doctrinal problem by suggesting that the soul can grow in grace and spiritual maturity away from God. This assumption is incompatible with the Reformation view that growth in grace can only take place in communion with God and through the direct activity of the Holy Spirit.

- According to Dr. Reeves, what is the litmus test of truly Reformed thought?

  Dr. Reeves offered a simple yet penetrating litmus test of Reformed thought and practice: Does it glorify humanity, human values, and human performance, or does it glorify God? This principle operates as the dividing line that distinguishes the Reformed faith from all other approaches to God.

- According to Reformation theology, what is the chief end, or defining purpose, of human existence? How can the study of key Reformation truths equip Christians to pursue this purpose?

  The theology of the Reformation points toward the truth that the chief end of man is to glorify and enjoy God in all of life and for all time. The theological system that emerged from the Reformation placed God back at the center of Christian belief and practice. In a world where the constant pull is toward man-centeredness, the truths of the Reformation redirect our focus toward our sovereign, majestic, and glorious God. Reclaiming the truths of Scripture alone, faith alone, grace alone, Christ alone, and glory to God alone can halt our man-centered tendency in its tracks and pull our hearts and minds back to their rightful focus on God.

REVIEW QUIZ

Lesson 8

1. **A.**
   Reflecting on Paul's command to rejoice in Philippians 4, the Puritan Richard Sibbes noted that rejoicing in heaven, serving God cheerfully, resisting temptation, suffering persecution with courage, and other duties of the Christian life all depend on being assured of salvation. Sibbes said that we must "know that we have a part in Christ and in God."

2. **C.**
   Question 52 of the Heidelberg Catechism asks, "What comfort is it to you that Christ will come to judge the living and the dead?" The answer describes the return of Christ to judge the earth as an event that brings present comfort in this life.

3. **C.**
   The doctrine of purgatory gave rise to a booming purgatory industry during the late Middle Ages. Examples of this industry include prayers and Masses on behalf of the dead, the formation of chantries to reduce the time wealthy patrons would spend in purgatory, and the sale of indulgences to shorten or completely eliminate the deceased's sojourn in purgatory. This industry preyed on the fears and ignorance of common people who wanted to assuage the torment they and their loved ones would experience after death.

4. **B.**
   The German friar Johann Tetzel was selling indulgences extensively in Luther's vicinity in 1517. Tetzel's blood-chilling marketing tactics stunned Luther into action, prompting him to compose his famous Ninety-Five Theses.

5. **B.**
   "The Dream of Gerontius," a poem composed by Cardinal John Henry Newman, presents a view of purgatory that is based on the assumption that the soul will best mature away from the presence of God, alone and longing for its absent Lord. This assumption is inconsistent with Scripture's teaching on the centrality of union with Christ to spiritual growth.

6. **D.**
   In describing "the secret of happiness and the secret of life," Calvin wrote, "The chief good of man is nothing else but union with God." The Westminster Shorter Catechism, written a century later, voiced a similar but slightly modified version of this statement when it affirmed that "man's chief end is to glorify God, and to enjoy Him forever."